SCOOBY-DOO!
WHERE ARE YOU

T0012195

SCOOBY-DOO EXPLORES
THE NEIGHBORHOOD

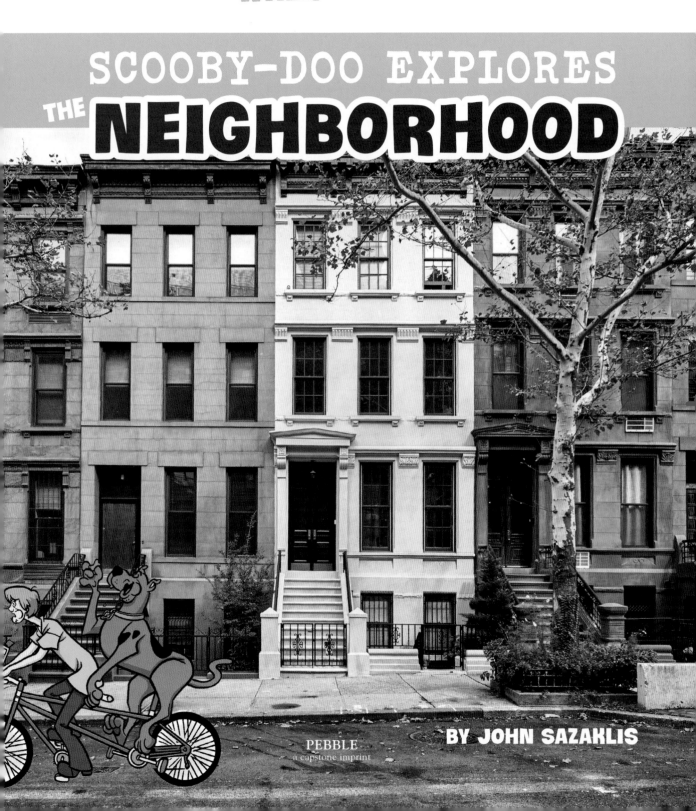

BY JOHN SAZAKLIS

PEBBLE
a capstone imprint

Published by Pebble, an imprint of Capstone
1710 Roe Crest Drive, North Mankato, Minnesota 56003
capstonepub.com

Library of Congress Cataloging-in-Publication Data is available on the Library of Congress website
ISBN: 9780756576257 (hardcover)
ISBN: 9780756576202 (paperback)
ISBN: 9780756576219 (ebook PDF)

Summary: Scooby-Doo and the Mystery Inc. gang learn about neighborhoods.

Editorial Credits
Editor: Christianne Jones; Designer: Bobbie Nuytten; Media Researcher: Rebekah Hubstenberger;
Production Specialist: Whitney Schaefer

Image Credits
Alamy: Len Collection, 19 (middle); Dreamstime: Julianne Geise, 17 (top right); Getty Images:
Alexander Spatari, 9 (top right), Allison Joyce, 15 (middle), alvarez, 29 (middle left), Brian
Kersey, 16, Caia Image, Cover (middle right), Cancan Chu, 15 (bottom), FrankvandenBergh,
22, Hulton Archive, 23 (middle), 31 (top), iStock/baona, 6, iStock/Dennis Swanson - Studio
101 West Photography, 21 (middle left), iStock/espiegle, 27 (top), iStock/felixmiziozonikov, 25
(middle left), iStock/Gregor Inkret, 7 (middle), iStock/niknikon, 21 (middle), iStock/scaliger, 26,
JGalione, 4 (top right), Justin Sullivan, 19 (bottom), Katrin Ray Shumakov, 3 (middle right), 24,
manonallard, 25 (top), martin-dm, 3 (bottom left), 20, MesquitaFMS, 25 (middle right), Olaf Kruger,
27 (bottom), Putu Sayoga, 15 (top), SolStock, 3 (bottom middle), 30, Spencer Platt, 17 (top left),
TommL, 2 (bottom left), 8, Topical Press Agency, 19 (top), WALTER ZERLA, 4 (bottom); Library
of Congress: Prints and Photographs Division, 11 (top); Shutterstock: Africa Studio, 11 (bottom),
Brian Goodman, Cover (top right), 1, Diane Bondareff, 13 (top right), DisobeyArt, 29 (top right),
Drazen Zigic, 13 (middle right), 29 (top left), hxdbzxy, 9 (top right), Igor Bukhlin, 10, Joni Hanebutt,
17 (middle), Josef Hanus, 2 (bottom right), 12, Ken Wolter, 18, Kira_Yan, Cover (middle right
background), kittirat roekburi, 28, Kzenon, 21 (top right), Lopolo, 14, MeganBrady, 27 (middle),
MirasWonderland, 23 (bottom), Niloo, 9 (middle right), Orhan Cam, 7 (top), Rawpixel.com, 13
Cover (bottom right), TongRoRo, 31 (middle), Viktoriia Hnatiuk, 9 (middle left), voronaman, 11
(middle), wavebreakmedia, 5 (middle); The New York Public Library: The Miriam and Ira D.
Wallach Division of Art, Prints and Photographs, 23 (top)

Printed and bound in China.   PO 5593

A NEW NEIGHBORHOOD

The Scooby-Doo gang is lost in a new neighborhood!

A neighborhood is a small area in a town or city where a group of people live. Some neighborhoods are big. Some are small. Some are old. Some are new.

Use the clues in the photos and text to guess each place the gang has discovered in the new community.

Scooby and Velma are in a building full of books. Looking for a spooky story or a mystery? An expert employee will lead the way. They will even let you borrow the books to read at home!

Velma delves into research on a computer.

Scooby is captivated by story time.

SCOOBY-DOO, WHERE ARE YOU?

WE ARE AT THE LIBRARY!

Dracula loves the library because he can sink his teeth into a good book!

Ruh-roh!

The largest library in the United States is the Library of Congress in Washington, D.C.

Built in 859, the Al-Qarawiyyin Library in Morocco is the oldest one still open for business.

Real bats live in the Joanina Library in Portugal. They eat insects that damage book pages.

Ruh-roh! Scooby's out of Scooby Snacks! Shaggy finds the perfect place to get some food. There are aisles and aisles filled with tasty treats and scrumptious snacks.

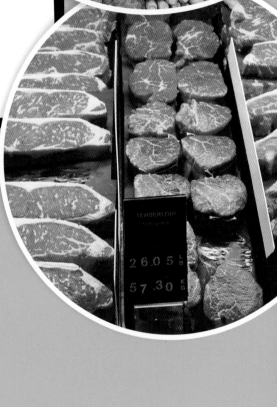

There are rows and rows of fruits and vegetables.

There is even a meat counter and a bakery section.

SCOOBY-DOO, WHERE ARE YOU?

WE ARE AT A SUPERMARKET!

Like, did you hear about the snowman looking for carrots? He was "picking" his nose!

Ree-hee-hee!

The Piggly Wiggly was the first supermarket in the world. It opened in 1916 in Memphis, Tennessee.

Self-service checkout lanes were invented in 1992.

The shopping cart was invented in 1937. It has many names around the world, including trolley and buggy.

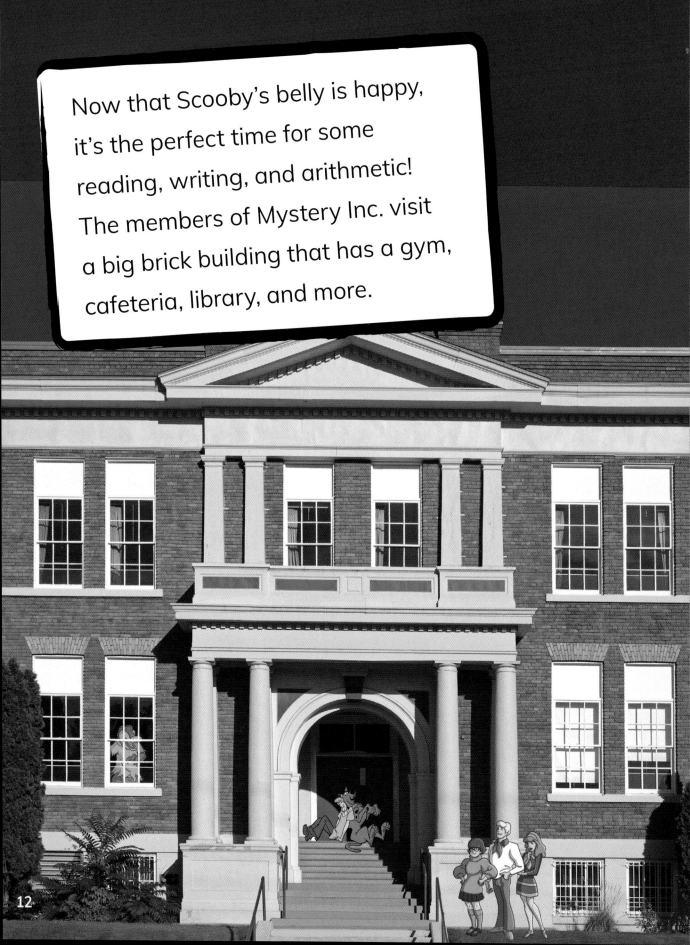

Now that Scooby's belly is happy, it's the perfect time for some reading, writing, and arithmetic! The members of Mystery Inc. visit a big brick building that has a gym, cafeteria, library, and more.

Lockers line the long hallways.

Flyers about robotics, sports, theater, and more activities fill the bulletin boards.

Classrooms are filled with eager students and excited teachers. They even voted Scooby to be teacher's pet!

SCOOBY-DOO, WHERE ARE YOU?

WE ARE AT SCHOOL!

Did you know this school haunted?

That's because it has a lot of school "spirit."

The Green School in Bali, Indonesia, is eco-friendly. It's made with bamboo, uses solar panels, and has a hydro-powered generator.

Bangladesh has big floods every year, so they have boat schools.

The Dongzhong Cave School in China was open from 1984–2011.

After school, the gang finds a place that's filled with letters and packages.

This busy place is a hub for all the mail in the neighborhood. If you need to send something, this is the place to be!

Fred buys stamps while Shaggy takes a new passport photo. **Smile!**

Apply for a
U.S. Passport
here.

Photos &
d Service
lable.

usps.com/passpo

UNITED
POST

SCOOBY-DOO, WHERE ARE YOU?

WE ARE AT THE POST OFFICE!

What has more letters than the alphabet?

Rhe Post Office!

The United States Post Office (USPS) Department was founded in 1775.

Owney the Dog became the unofficial mascot of the U.S. Post Office in 1888.

Millions of pieces of mail are collected, sorted, and delivered every day by the U.S. Postal Service.

DING! DING! DING! As Scooby and his friends leave the post office, they hear an alarm. It's a call to action for trained people who help in emergencies.

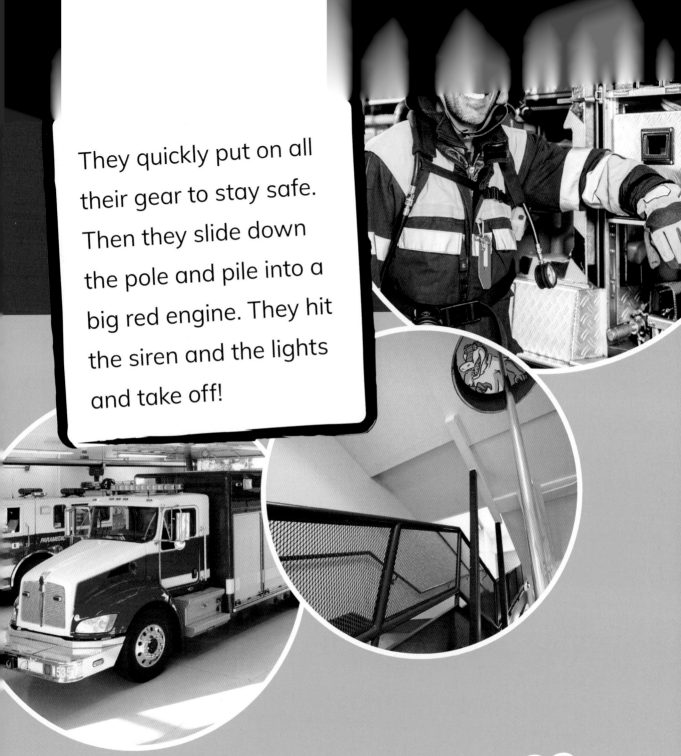

They quickly put on all their gear to stay safe. Then they slide down the pole and pile into a big red engine. They hit the siren and the lights and take off!

SCOOBY-DOO, WHERE ARE YOU?

WE ARE AT THE FIRE STATION!

22

Benjamin Franklin established the first fire company in 1736.

From 1870 to 1920, fire engines were pulled by horses.

Dalmatians helped firefighters with their ability to calm horses. They are considered the mascots of fire houses.

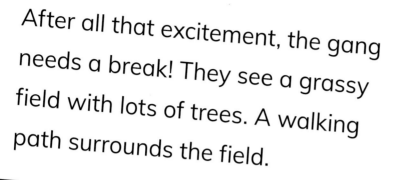

After all that excitement, the gang needs a break! They see a grassy field with lots of trees. A walking path surrounds the field.

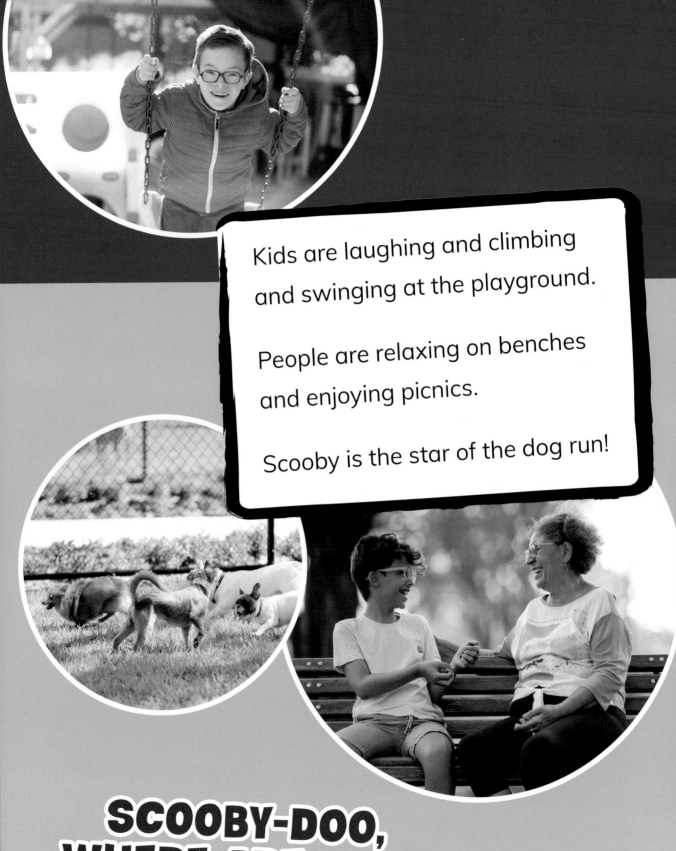

Kids are laughing and climbing and swinging at the playground.

People are relaxing on benches and enjoying picnics.

Scooby is the star of the dog run!

SCOOBY-DOO,
WHERE ARE YOU?

WE ARE AT THE PARK!

Even though it's in New York City, Central Park is bigger than some countries.

In 1872, Yellowstone Park in Wyoming became the first national park in the world.

Greenland's National Park is the world's largest.

Sniff! Sniff! A delicious smell wafts into the park, and Shaggy and Scooby eagerly follow it.

Sparkling lights glow over a packed patio.

Tables and booths are filled with families and friends.

Waiters rush around taking orders and delivering food and drinks.

SCOOBY-DOO, WHERE ARE YOU?

WE ARE AT A RESTAURANT!

What did the waiter say to the skeleton?

"Bone" appétit!

Many believe the first "modern" restaurant opened in 1765 in Paris.

The Union Oyster House in Boston is the oldest restaurant in the United States. It has been open since 1826.

White Castle was the first fast food restaurant chain. It opening in 1921.

Scooby-Doo and the Mystery Inc. gang explored every corner of a new neighborhood, but they weren't alone! The Gator Ghoul wanted to explore a new neighborhood too! Look through the book again and spot him hiding in each location.

ABOUT THE AUTHOR

John Sazaklis is a *New York Times* bestselling author with almost 100 children's books under his utility belt! He has also illustrated Spider-Man books, created toys for MAD magazine, and written for the BEN 10 animated series. John lives in New York City with his superpowered wife and daughter.